We're The Same, We're Different
and We All Belong

A Social Emotional Learning (SEL) Book for Kids about Diversity, Kindness, Race and Empathy

by
KayJay Miller

Copyright © 2023 by KayJay Miller

All rights reserved. Published in the United States by Force For Good Media LLC, Los Angeles.
Thank you for purchasing this book and welcome to the Force For Good Media family!
For all inquiries, please drop us a line at: hello@F4GM.com
For more of our books, visit us at www.ForceForGoodMedia.com

Publisher's Cataloging-in-Publication data

Names: Miller, KayJay, author.

Title: We're the same, we're different and we all belong : a social emotional learning (SEL) book for kids about diversity, kindness, race & empathy / by KayJay Miller.

Description: Los Angeles, California : Force For Good Media LLC, [2023] | Series: We all belong ; book 1. | Audience: 3 – 7 years old. | Summary: In her own heartwarming, hilarious words, Marnie, a spunky multiracial kindergartener, explores the concept of diversity. She finds that differences (e.g. race, size, accent, learning styles, ways of moving around etc.) are only one part of a person's unique story.--Publisher.

Identifiers: ISBN: 978-1-961930-02-5 (Hardcover) | 978-1-961930-00-1 (Paperback) | 978-1-961930-01-8 (Kindle) | 978-1-961930-06-3 (Epub) | 978-1-961930-04-9 (Audio-book) | LCCN: 2023913084

Subjects: CYAC: Individual differences--Fiction. | Difference--Fiction. | Self-esteem--Fiction. | Identity--Fiction. | Friendship--Fiction. | Race awareness--Fiction. | Prejudices--Fiction. | Toleration--Fiction. | Kindness--Fiction. | Empathy--Fiction. | Life skills--Fiction. | United States--Race relations--Fiction. | Racism--United States--Fiction. | African American children--Fiction. | Hispanic Americans--Fiction. | Racially mixed people--Fiction. | Cultural pluralism--Fiction. | Children with disabilities--Fiction. | Neurodiversity--Fiction. | Children of immigrants--Fiction.

Classification: LCC: PZ7.1.M5814 W47 2023 | DDC: [E]--dc23

First Edition

WHO am I?

My name is
Marnie.

I am six years old.

That means
I'm basically a
big girl now.

I'm kind of a **big deal.**

Mama says everyone has a story.

We're like books with lots of pages.

With different parts that make up who we are.

All the parts and pages, when you put them together, make us **unique.**

Unique means **different** and **special.**

Like no one else in the world.

So, I'm not just:
a girl named Marnie who is 3¾ feet tall,
who likes **pink sparkles**,
and **cats**,
and **star-shaped crackers**.

I am me.

If you're **big** or **small**.

If you have **your own way of learning things.**

If it's the **shape of your eyes** or the **glasses** you wear.

If it's **your clothes** or **your hairstyle**.

If it's the **way you speak**.

If it's **the food you eat**.

If you use a **wheelchair** or **crutches** to get around—

Well, those are **all just parts of your story**.

Another part of everyone's story is the
color of our skin and
where our family comes from.

Mama is **black.** Her family is from Jamaica and Cuba.

Daddy is **white.** His family is from the United States of America (and, before that, Italy and Poland).

No one is really the actual color black or the actual color white.

My skin is the color of **Mama's banana bread.**

Your skin might be the color of

coffee brown chocolate

or

golden, beige fudge

or

milky, peachy cream.

What do you look like?

Uniquely You

My hair is **beautiful** and **thick** and **curly.**

I can do **so many cool hairstyles**—

cornrows, twists, afro-puffs, a ballerina bun, box braids and more.

Or, I can just set it free.

My big, pretty afro.

All those curls.

I love my hair!

What do you like to do with your hair?

Once I went to a new school and some of the children **treated me differently** because...

to them, **my skin color was different** and my **hair was different** too.

They said they didn't want to play with me because of it.

Some kids said mean things about the color of my skin and the way my hair is.

When I told Mama, she said,
"We're the same, we're different
and we all belong."

Being different doesn't make
someone weird,
it just makes them different.

And be nice to them because,
to them, **you are different too!**

We may seem **soooooooo
different...** but deep down,
we're kind of the same.

The things people **can see...** are **NOT the only things** you are.

I'm going to answer some questions on the next few pages. I hope you'll answer them too.

That way, **you'll get to know me.** And **I'll get to know you.**

I like **playing with my dolls** even if I've cut their hair off and fed them so much food they smell like egg sandwiches and tuna!

I like **funny books.**

Riding my bike.

And **animals.**

And, sometimes, saying bathroom potty words (sorry Mama!).

What do you love to do?

One time I was showing off to my two best friends, Nicolette and Ekow.

I climbed up the monkey bars. **Right to the top.** It was so high up. My heart was thumping. **I couldn't move.**

Thought I was going to fall.

I was so scared **and I did it anyway.**

I realized I can do hard things!

What's the scariest thing you've ever done?

If a magical genie gave me one wish...

I'd get my dream cat.
Friendly and fluffy with fur
like a teddy bear.
And I'd call her **Joey Sparkle**.

> **If a genie gave you one wish, what would you ask for?**

My **favorite joke** right now is:

What's the name for a fairy who doesn't like to bathe?

Stinkerbell!

Sometimes, I tell jokes and no one laughs but I always find them funny.

What is your favorite joke?

When I grow up, **I want to be...**

I don't know. Yet.

Maybe a **superhero**.

Or a **doctor for animals.**
I love animals.

Or a **dancer in carnival** in the Caribbean.
I love to dance with sunlight on my face!

Oh, and a doctor for animals is a vet.
I might be a vet.

What do you want to be when you grow up?

I love my cool fashion.

I choose it myself.

I love my shake-my-bottom dance.

And my bravery.
I used to be scared to try new things.

But now,

I say, "I can't do it YET," and
"Mistakes help me learn,"

and telling myself that helps me
to do hard things.

What do you love about yourself?

After all these questions, we're not strangers anymore.
I feel like you really know me!

I'm so **grateful** and **happy** we took the time to find out about each other.

I can't wait to
hang out again soon!

Love,

Your new friend,

Marnie

xox

KayJay Miller - author

KayJay Miller has been... a Caribbean child dancing in full carnival costume, an Oxford student cycling everywhere and an award-winning writer (theater, film and children's TV). She is now Mom to an amazing, cheeky five-year-old and an author of kids' books that are a force for good.

KayJay's funny, touching kids' books help parents and educators bond more deeply with their children while helping them to become the best they can be (socially and emotionally).

Her very first children's book was written when she was eighteen years old as a love letter to her adorable twin sisters who were five years old and thousands of miles away. She wanted them to know that they would always be loved by her, no matter how far away she was.

To claim your FREE gift, visit:
www.F4GM.com/SameDifferent

We have a feeling
you're going to love it!

Thanks for buying this book
and welcome to the
Force For Good Media family!

About Us

At Force For Good Media, our mission is to help teach children the important Social and Emotional Learning (SEL) life lessons they need. We create meaningful, entertaining, educational stories that help children become the best version of themselves. Parents and children get the chance to bond even more deeply when they read these stories together.

Made in the USA
Middletown, DE
10 October 2023